Let Go and Let God for Marriage:

You Can't Change Your Spouse (But God Can)

Steve and Leigh Baumann, Bill and Trudy Hehn

SOUTHERN LIGHTS, DIVISION OF SEASCAPE PRESS

Copyright © 2025 by Steve & Leigh Baumann and Bill & Trudy Hehn

Copyright Southern Lights Press, A Division of Seascape Press. All rights reserved. No part of this publication may be reproduced, stored in a retrieval system, or transmitted in any form or by any means—electronic, mechanical, photocopy, recording, or otherwise—without prior written permission of the publisher, except for brief quotations in critical reviews or articles.

Scripture Quotations:
Scripture quotations are taken from the New Revised Standard Version Bible. For Catholic readers, the NRSV Catholic Edition is fully equivalent.

Scripture quotations are from the *New Revised Standard Version Bible*, copyright © 1989, Division of Christian Education of the National Council of the Churches of Christ in the United States of America. Used by permission. All rights reserved worldwide.

Published by:
Southern Lights Press
A Division of Seascape Press
Waverly, Georgia 31565
www.southernlightspress.com

ISBN – 978-0-9769510-0-1 (paperback)
ISBN – 978-0-9769510-3-2 (ebook)

Contents

1. THE TRUTH ABOUT MARRIAGE — 1
2. HOW TO USE THIS BOOK — 5
3. TRYING TO CHANGE YOUR SPOUSE — 12
4. HOUSEHOLD PARTNERSHIP AND CONTROL — 15
5. COMMITMENT AND FOLLOW-THROUGH — 19
6. FINANCIAL HABITS AND PRIORITIES — 22
7. RELATIONSHIP WITH FAMILY AND PARENTING — 25
8. CAREER AND AMBITION — 29
9. TOGETHERNESS AS A COUPLE — 32
10. HEALTH AND HABITS — 35
11. PAST HURTS AND EMOTIONAL HEALING — 38
12. NEEDS AND EXPECTATIONS — 41

13.	PACE OF CHANGE IN YOUR MARRIAGE	44
14.	RESPONSE TO YOUR LOVE AND AFFECTION	47
15.	COMMUNICATION AND CONFLICT RESOLUTION	50
16.	PHYSICAL INTIMACY	53
17.	ADDICTIONS OR DESTRUCTIVE HABITS	56
18.	EMOTIONS AND MENTAL HEALTH	59
19.	TECHNOLOGY AND SOCIAL MEDIA BOUNDARIES	62
20.	FORGIVENESS AND HEALING FROM HURTS	66
21.	TEMPTATIONS AND FIDELITY	69
22.	LIFE PURPOSE AND CALLING	72
23.	TRIALS AND CHALLENGES	75
24.	INTEGRITY AND REPUTATION	78
25.	ATTITUDE AND OUTLOOK	81
26.	ANGER AND FRUSTRATION	84
27.	RELATIONSHIP WITH GOD	87
28.	PAST MISTAKES	90
29.	SELF-WORTH AND IDENTITY	94
30.	ROLE IN THE HOME	97

31.	TRUST AND TRUSTWORTHINESS	100
32.	LEGACY AND IMPACT	103
33.	YOUR NEW WAY OF LOVING	106
34.	THE RED THREAD	111
35.	ABOUT THE AUTHORS	113

THE TRUTH ABOUT MARRIAGE

You Can't Change Your Spouse (But God Can)

There comes a moment in every marriage when you realize that all your talking, pleading, suggesting, and strategizing has accomplished exactly nothing. You've tried reason. You've tried romance. You've tried ultimatums and you've tried silence. Yet your spouse remains stubbornly, frustratingly unchanged.

This moment of complete helplessness is actually a gift.

It's the moment when you discover what countless couples before you have learned: prayer is the only thing that always works. Not because prayer is magic, but because prayer does something profound that no amount of human effort can accomplish—it takes you straight to the Source of all transformation.

Here's what we've discovered in our years of working with struggling marriages: the safeguard you have with prayer is that you have to go through God to do it. You cannot approach the throne of grace with a bad attitude, wrong thinking, or incorrect motives and expect God to rubber-stamp your agenda. When you truly pray for your spouse, something remarkable happens—God begins to reveal anything in your own personality that is resistant to His order of things.

This is why prayer succeeds where conversation fails. When you talk to your spouse about change, you're operating from your own perspective, your own timeline, your own definition of what needs fixing. But when you pray, you're inviting the One who created your spouse to work in ways you never could imagine. You're acknowledging that the heart you're trying to reach belongs to Him, not you.

Prayer forces you to confront an uncomfortable truth: you cannot change another human being. You can influence, encourage, and inspire, but the deep work of transformation happens in a place only God can reach. The moment you truly accept this limitation is the moment you discover unlimited power—not your power, but His.

When you begin to pray earnestly for your spouse, God starts with you. He reveals the pride that makes you think you know better than Him. He exposes the impatience that refuses to trust His timing. He uncovers the fear that drives your need to control. Before He changes your spouse's heart, He purifies the heart that's doing the asking.

This is not a book about getting God to fix your spouse. This is a book about partnering with God to create the kind of marriage that brings Him glory—starting with your own surrender. It's about discovering that the very act of releasing control actually gives you access to a power far greater than any manipulation, argument, or strategy you could devise.

Every day that follows will ask you to do two things: let go of something you've been trying to control, and let God work in a way only He can. You'll find that as you release your grip on your spouse's choices, habits, and growth, you create space for the Holy Spirit to move in ways that will amaze you.

The prayer at the end of each day is not a formula for getting what you want. It's a pathway to wanting what God wants. And what God wants for your marriage is far better than anything you could orchestrate on your own.

Your spouse's transformation is God's responsibility. Your transformation is His invitation. The moment you accept both truths, everything changes—starting with you.

What "Letting Go" Really Means

Before we go any further, let's clear up a dangerous misconception. When we talk about "letting go and letting God" in your marriage, we're not suggesting you become a passive doormat who ignores problems, avoids difficult conversations, or abandons your responsibilities as a spouse. We're not advocating for spiritual negligence disguised as surrender.

Real "letting go" is actually the most active, courageous thing you can do. It means you continue to love well, communicate clearly, set healthy boundaries, and fulfill your marriage vows—but you do it all while releasing your stranglehold on the outcomes. You pray fervently while acting wisely. You speak truth in love while trusting God to open ears that only He can open. You model the character you long to see while releasing the burden of being your spouse's Holy Spirit.

Think of it this way: a skilled gardener doesn't plant seeds and then ignore them. They water consistently, provide proper nutrients, remove weeds, and create the best possible environment for growth. But they don't stand over the plant demanding it grow faster, trying to force buds to bloom, or digging up roots to check their progress. They do their part faithfully and trust the mysterious process of life to do what only it can do.

In marriage, letting go means you become the most loving, praying, intentional spouse you can be while surrendering the timeline and the methods of your spouse's transformation to the only One who can actually change a human heart. You stop trying to be their change agent and start being their greatest champion in prayer.

This is not giving up on your marriage—it's giving your marriage the greatest possible chance to become everything God intended it to be.

HOW TO USE THIS BOOK

Understanding the Sacred Chorus

This Let Go and Let God book is designed as a daily journey, with each chapter offering a complete devotional experience for one day. However, this is not a rigid calendar—you may read the days in order as a sequential journey, or you may find yourself drawn to specific days that speak to your current situation. Many readers discover that certain chapters become touchstones they return to repeatedly, each reading revealing new layers of wisdom and comfort.

This flexibility is intentional. Marriage is not a linear experience, and neither should be your spiritual support. Some days you may need the gentle release offered in one chapter, while other days call for the bold trust explored in another. Allow yourself the freedom to be led by your heart and circumstances to the message you most need to hear.

The Sacred Chorus: Four Divine Voices

Each daily chapter unfolds through four distinct voices, creating what we call a "sacred chorus"—a harmonious blend of divine perspectives that addresses both your mind and your heart, your struggles and your hopes. These voices represent different aspects of God's character and different ways the divine intersects with human experience.

Mary: Let Go (Maternal Wisdom and Sacred Release)

Mary's voice in the "Let Go" section offers something uniquely powerful—the wisdom of one who has faced the ultimate surrender and found it to be the pathway to the ultimate blessing. For readers from traditions that pray to Mary, she speaks as the compassionate mother who intercedes for her children, understanding your struggles and petitioning on your behalf. For readers from traditions that don't pray to Mary, she represents the embodiment of feminine wisdom, maternal intuition, and the grace of sacred surrender.

Mary knows what it means to release control over someone you love more than life itself. She watched her son face misunderstanding, rejection, and ultimately death, all while trusting that God's plan was working even when it made no earthly sense. Her voice carries the authority of one who has walked the path of radical trust and found it leads to resurrection.

Her words are often the most challenging because they invite you to release your grip on outcomes, people, and timelines that feel essential to your happiness. Yet they are also the most freeing, because they come from one who discovered that letting go is not losing—it's making space for miracles.

The Father: Let God (Gentle Authority and Loving Protection)

When the Father speaks in the "Let God" section, His voice carries the weight of ultimate authority tempered by infinite love. This is not the harsh voice of judgment, but the steady presence of a wise Father who sees the end from the beginning. He speaks with the calm confidence of One who is never surprised by human struggle and never lacking in solutions.

The Father's voice invites you to trust—not blindly, but with the assurance that comes from knowing you are held by hands that are both powerful enough to change any situation and tender enough to handle your fragile hopes. His words often challenge your assumptions about control while simultaneously offering the security that comes from surrendering to One whose plans are always redemptive.

The Holy Spirit: Prayer for Your Spouse and Questions for the Heart (Activating Grace)

The Holy Spirit's presence manifests in the "Prayer for Your Spouse" and "Questions for the Heart" sections, where your own voice becomes the vessel for divine intercession. This is where the miraculous intersection occurs—your human words, emotions, and desires are breathed through by divine wind, creating prayers that are simultaneously deeply personal and profoundly powerful.

The Spirit works through your authentic self, not despite it. Your fears, hopes, frustrations, and dreams become the raw material through which the Spirit crafts prayers that align with God's heart. This voice acknowledges that you don't always know what to pray or how to pray it, but the Spirit does—and is willing to pray through you with groanings too deep for words.

Jesus: Prayer for You (The Walking Companion)

Jesus speaks as your intimate friend and understanding companion in the "Prayer for You" section. His voice is perhaps the most accessible because He alone among the divine persons has walked in human shoes, felt the sting of betrayal, experienced the weight of unmet expectations, and knows the complexity of loving imperfect people in an imperfect world.

When Jesus prays for you, His words carry both divine power and human understanding. He speaks as one who has been tempted yet remained faithful, who has been misunderstood yet continued loving, who has been disappointed yet never grew bitter. His prayers for you are not distant theological pronouncements but intimate conversations between friends—one who understands exactly what you're facing and has the power to help you through it.

The Intentional Design: Why These Voices Matter

The selection and assignment of these voices is not arbitrary but flows from deep theological reflection and practical wisdom about how transformation actually occurs in human hearts. Each voice addresses a different aspect of the surrender and trust process:

Mary calls you to release what you were never meant to carry. Her maternal wisdom recognizes when you've been trying to do God's job and gently but firmly guides you back to your proper place as beloved child, not puppet master.

The Father assures you of His capability to handle what you've released. His voice provides the security and confidence needed to actually let go—not into a void, but into hands that are infinitely more capable than your own.

The Spirit empowers your participation in the process through prayer for your spouse that is both human and divine. This voice acknowledges that surrender is not passive but requires active cooperation with grace. The scripture reflects the Living Word.

Jesus provides the relational bridge that makes the whole process feel safe and personal. His voice reminds you that this is not about abstract theological concepts but about relationship—with Him and through Him with others.

A Universal Language of the Heart

These voices have been crafted to speak to the universal human experience of love, loss, hope, and surrender that transcends denominational boundaries. Whether you come from a tradition rich in liturgy and sacrament or one that emphasizes personal relationship and Scripture, whether you've prayed the rosary since childhood or have recently discovered prayer through contemporary worship, these voices will feel both familiar and fresh.

The goal is not theological uniformity but spiritual unity—recognition that all who love God and struggle with loving people imperfectly are part of the same family, facing the same challenges, and in need of the same grace. Mary's voice will resonate with some readers as intercessor and with others as example, but for all, she represents the possibility of trusting God even when His plans don't match your preferences.

An Invitation to Depth

Each voice has been carefully cultivated to offer not just comfort but transformation, not just sympathy but solution, not just understanding but empowerment. As you read, you may find that different voices speak more clearly to you at different times. Some days, Mary's gentle release may be exactly what your control-weary heart needs to hear. Other days, the Father's confident declarations may provide the stability your anxious mind requires.

Allow yourself to be surprised by which voice ministers most deeply to you on any given day. Let yourself argue with the voices when their challenges feel too difficult, sit with their comfort when their grace feels too good to be true, and rest in their wisdom when your own understanding reaches its limits.

This is more than a book—it's a conversation with the divine family that has been loving people through marriage struggles since the beginning of time. You are invited not just to read these voices but to enter into a relationship with them, allowing their distinct perspectives to shape not only how you approach your marriage challenges but how you understand yourself as a beloved child of God.

Welcome to the sacred chorus. Your part in this divine conversation matters, and your willingness to listen—and ultimately to "Let Go and Let God"—has the power to transform not only your marriage but your understanding of how love actually works in a broken but redeemable world.

TRYING TO CHANGE YOUR SPOUSE

Day 1

Let Go: Stop believing you can fix, improve, or transform your spouse through nagging, criticism, or manipulation. Release the exhausting burden of being their Holy Spirit.

Let God: God sees every area where your spouse needs growth, and He has a perfect plan for their transformation. He knows exactly what experiences, people, and circumstances will speak to their heart. His love for your spouse is deeper than yours, and His methods are far more effective than anything you could devise. When you step back, you create space for the Holy Spirit to work in ways that penetrate the heart rather than just change behavior.

Scripture: *"I am confident of this, that the one who began a good work among you will bring it to completion by the day of Jesus Christ."* - Philippians 1:6

Prayer for Your Spouse: *"Lord, I place my spouse completely in Your hands. You know every area where they need to grow, every wound that needs healing, every strength that needs developing. Do in their heart what only You can do. Open their eyes to truth, soften their heart to Your leading, and shape them into the person You created them to be. I trust Your timing, Your methods, and Your love for them. Work in ways I could never imagine. In Jesus' name, Amen."*

Questions for the Heart:

What specific behaviors or attitudes in my spouse trigger my need to control or fix them, and how can I surrender these areas to God?

Where am I acting as their Holy Spirit instead of trusting the real Holy Spirit to work in their life?

What fears drive my need to change my spouse, and how can God help me find security in Him instead?

How can God transform my heart to love my spouse unconditionally while they are on their own journey of growth?

Prayer for You: *"My precious child, I see how exhausted you are from trying to be what only I can be in your spouse's life. You were never meant to carry the weight of another person's transformation. That burden belongs to Me alone, and I am more than capable of bearing it.*

I know your heart's desire for your spouse to grow and change comes from love, but I want to free you from the frustration and disap-

pointment that comes from trying to do My job. When you release your spouse into My hands, you're not giving up—you're finally allowing Me to work in ways your human efforts never could.

Trust Me with the person you love most. I see their heart more clearly than you do, and I love them even more deeply than you can imagine. While you see their flaws and long for change, I see their potential and have already begun the good work that I will faithfully complete.

Rest in My perfect timing and trust My perfect methods. Your role is to love, pray, and surrender. My role is to transform. Let Me do what I do best while you find peace in what I've called you to do. Your marriage will flourish when you stop trying to be their creator and instead trust their Creator.

Be still and watch Me work miracles in ways that will amaze you."

HOUSEHOLD PARTNERSHIP AND CONTROL

Day 2

Let Go: Stop trying to control both the decisions and the execution of household management. Release the need to micromanage how things are done, who does what, and when tasks are completed. Stop nagging about chores, criticizing their methods, or keeping score of contributions. Release the exhausting burden of being both the household decision-maker and task supervisor.

Let God: God can give your spouse wisdom for household decisions and inspire them to contribute as a true partner. He can soften stubborn hearts about both planning and participation, creating willingness to collaborate in decision-making and take initiative in household tasks. The Holy Spirit can convict them when they're being selfish, lazy, or leaving too much responsibility on you, and inspire them to seek unity in both planning and executing home management. God can help them see how their actions (or lack of action) affect the entire family and create in them a servant's heart that naturally looks for ways to help and contribute.

Scripture: *"Do nothing from selfish ambition or conceit, but in humility regard others as better than yourselves. Let each of you look not to your own interests, but to the interests of others."* - Philippians 2:3-4

Prayer for Your Spouse: *"Lord, give my spouse wisdom in our household decisions and a servant's heart in our home. Help them see what needs to be done and take initiative rather than waiting to be asked. When we disagree about household choices, work in their heart to create a spirit of cooperation and compromise. Remove any selfishness or stubbornness that prevents partnership. Create in them a desire to be a true collaborator in both planning and caring for our home and family. Help them see and appreciate the work I do, and motivate them to contribute willingly and cheerfully. Make us a team that honors You in both our decisions and our daily tasks. Amen."*

Questions for the Heart:

What household decisions or standards am I most unwilling to compromise on, and how does my need for control create tension rather than partnership?

Where am I keeping score of contributions instead of appreciating different ways my spouse serves our family?

How do my attempts to manage both planning and execution rob my spouse of opportunities to step up and contribute?

What would it look like to truly collaborate in household management instead of controlling both the decisions and the tasks?

Prayer for You: *"My dear child, I see how much you carry in both planning and managing your household. You feel responsible for making the right decisions AND ensuring everything gets done properly, but this double burden was never meant for one person to bear alone.*

I gave you a partner to share both the mental load of household management and the physical work of maintaining your home. When you control both the decision-making and the execution, you rob your spouse of the opportunity to truly partner with you and rob yourself of the support I intended you to have.

Your spouse may contribute differently than you do or have ideas you haven't considered. Their methods may not match yours, but that doesn't make them wrong. I can work in their heart to develop both wisdom for decisions and initiative for tasks far more effectively than your management can.

Release your grip on both the planning and the doing. Trust Me to guide you both as partners who bring different strengths to your household. Create an atmosphere of appreciation and teamwork rather than criticism and control. Your home will be more peaceful when you focus on collaboration rather than domination.

Let Me develop in your spouse both a heart for wise decisions and willing hands for household tasks. Trust that I can create true partnership in both areas."

COMMITMENT AND FOLLOW-THROUGH

Day 3

Let Go: Stop trying to force them to keep commitments through nagging, reminding, or managing their responsibilities. Release frustration when they don't follow through on promises or plans.

Let God: God can develop in your spouse the character qualities of reliability, perseverance, and integrity that make commitment natural rather than forced. The Holy Spirit can convict them about the importance of keeping their word and following through on promises. God can heal whatever drives their pattern of uncommitted behavior—whether it's fear, selfishness, or past wounds—and create in them a deep desire to be someone whose word can be trusted completely.

Scripture: *"Let your word be 'Yes, Yes' or 'No, No'; anything more than this comes from the evil one."* - Matthew 5:37

Prayer for Your Spouse: *"Lord, work in my spouse's heart to create genuine commitment and follow-through. Help them understand that their word is their bond and that broken promises damage our relationship and their character. Give them the strength to keep commitments even when it's difficult or inconvenient. Heal whatever drives their pattern of not following through, and create in them a desire to be completely reliable. Help them see how their consistency affects our trust and intimacy. Amen."*

Questions for the Heart:

What commitments or promises from my spouse matter most to me, and how do I react when they don't follow through?

Where am I trying to force their commitment instead of allowing natural consequences to teach them?

How does their pattern of unreliability affect my willingness to make plans or trust their word?

What would it look like to express my needs clearly while allowing them to choose their level of commitment without my management?

Prayer for You: *"Beloved, I understand how frustrating it is when your spouse doesn't follow through on commitments or keep the promises they make. You've learned not to count on their word, and this creates distance and disappointment in your relationship.*

Your spouse's struggle with commitment may stem from various issues—being overwhelmed, lacking organization skills, fear of failure, or simply not understanding how their unreliability affects you. These patterns require My intervention in their heart, not your management of their behavior.

When you constantly remind, nag, or try to force follow-through, you often create resentment rather than reliability. True commitment must come from their own character and their love for you, not from external pressure.

I can work in their heart to help them understand how precious their word should be and how their reliability affects your trust. I can give them practical wisdom about managing commitments and the character strength to follow through even when it's difficult.

Stop being their external conscience and start allowing natural consequences to teach them. When they don't follow through, let them experience the results rather than rescuing them. Express your disappointment honestly but don't take responsibility for managing their commitments.

Trust Me to develop reliability in them while you focus on taking care of yourself and not depending on promises they're not ready to keep. I can create genuine commitment in their heart that will surprise you."

FINANCIAL HABITS AND PRIORITIES

Day 4

Let Go: Stop trying to control every spending decision or impose your financial fears on your spouse. Release anxiety about money matters that are beyond your individual control.

Let God: God is your ultimate provider, and He can work in your spouse's heart to create wisdom, contentment, and proper priorities with money. He can convict them of unwise spending patterns, create gratitude for what you have, and inspire generosity and stewardship. The same God who owns cattle on a thousand hills can teach your spouse to trust Him with finances and find security in His provision rather than in accumulating things.

Scripture: *"And my God will fully satisfy every need of yours according to his riches in glory in Christ Jesus."* - Philippians 4:19

Prayer for Your Spouse: *"Provider God, You know our financial needs and my spouse's relationship with money. Work in their heart to create wisdom in spending, contentment with what we have, and trust in Your provision. If there are areas of financial sin or foolishness, convict them gently but clearly. Help them find their security in You, not in things. Teach them to be a good steward of what You've given us. Supply our needs according to Your riches. Amen."*

Questions for the Heart:

What financial fears or past experiences drive my need to control our money decisions, and how can I surrender these anxieties to God?

Where am I trusting in money and financial security more than I'm trusting in God's provision?

How do my attempts to control our finances create tension and conflict instead of unity in our marriage?

What would it look like to truly partnership with my spouse in financial stewardship instead of trying to be the sole financial manager?

Prayer for You: *"My child, I see the worry that keeps you awake at night counting dollars and calculating what-ifs. I know that money feels like security in an uncertain world, but I want you to find your security in Me, not in bank account balances or perfect budgets.*

Your attempts to control every financial decision come from love and concern for your family's welfare, but they often create the very stress and conflict you're trying to prevent. When you grip finances so tightly, you leave no room for Me to provide in ways that might surprise you.

I am your Provider, and I have never failed to care for those who trust Me. I fed five thousand with a boy's lunch. I made oil and flour multiply for a desperate widow. I can make your resources stretch further than your mathematics can calculate, and I can open doors of opportunity you never saw coming.

Release your financial fears into My hands. Work together with your spouse as partners in stewardship, not adversaries in a battle for control. Seek My wisdom together, pray over your decisions together, and trust that I will guide you both as you honor Me with your resources.

The cattle on a thousand hills are Mine, and I delight in caring for My children. Let Me be your financial security."

RELATIONSHIP WITH FAMILY AND PARENTING

Day 5

Let Go: Stop trying to control how your spouse interacts with their family members or how they parent your children. Release the need to dictate their approach to family relationships, defend your family when they're wrong, or criticize their parenting style. Stop trying to win family loyalty battles or force identical approaches to family interactions.

Let God: God understands complex family dynamics better than anyone, and He can work in your spouse's heart to create healthy boundaries, wisdom in parenting, and healing in difficult relationships. He can give them discernment about toxic patterns, courage to address dysfunction, and wisdom to honor their parents while protecting your marriage. The Holy Spirit can heal generational wounds, break unhealthy family cycles, and guide them in raising your children with the right balance of love and discipline. God can use your spouse's unique gifts in both family relationships and parenting in ways you might not expect.

Scripture: *"For this reason a man will leave his father and mother and be joined to his wife, and the two will become one flesh."* - Ephesians 5:31

Prayer for Your Spouse: *"Lord, give my spouse wisdom in all their family relationships. Help them establish healthy boundaries that protect our marriage while still honoring their parents. If we have children, guide them in parenting with the right balance of love and discipline, and help them see each child's unique needs. Heal any wounds from their family of origin that affect our relationship. Give them courage to address dysfunction and wisdom to know when to engage and when to step back. Break any generational patterns that don't honor You, and help them prioritize our marriage covenant. Use their unique gifts to bless our family unit. Amen."*

Questions for the Heart:

What family conflicts, loyalty battles, or parenting decisions am I trying to control that are actually between my spouse and their family members or children?

How do my attempts to manage family dynamics or criticize their parenting create additional stress rather than the unity I'm seeking?

Where am I expecting my spouse to handle family relationships or parent exactly like me instead of trusting God to use their unique approach?

What boundaries do I need to establish for myself while allowing my spouse to navigate their family relationships and parenting responsibilities with God's guidance?

Prayer for You: "*My beloved, I see how much you care about family relationships and want harmony in your home. Whether it's watching your spouse struggle with difficult family dynamics or disagreeing with their parenting approach, your heart wants what's best for everyone involved. But your attempts to control these relationships often create division rather than the unity you desire.*

Family wounds run deep, and healing is complex. Your spouse may be working through years of complicated emotions and relationships in ways that don't make sense to you. If you have children, your spouse brings unique gifts and perspectives to parenting that complement yours, even when they seem different from your approach.

You cannot heal your spouse's family relationships, change generational patterns, or force them to parent exactly like you do. These are sacred journeys that each person must walk with Me at their own pace. What you see as weakness might actually be strength your family needs.

Your role is to love your spouse well in the midst of family struggles, provide a safe haven in your marriage, and pray for wisdom about when to speak and when to remain silent. Trust Me to work in their heart about unhealthy patterns and give them courage for difficult conversations when they're ready.

If you have children, they're watching how you and your spouse work together, learning about marriage, respect, and partnership from what they observe. When you criticize or undermine your spouse, you're teaching lessons you don't intend.

Focus on making your marriage a place of peace and healing. Let Me handle the extended family dynamics and guide your spouse in parenting while you concentrate on loving them through the process. I am working in every relationship, even the most difficult ones."

CAREER AND AMBITION

Day 6

Let Go: Stop trying to manage their career choices, push them toward your vision of success, or rescue them from work stress. Release your timeline for their professional growth.

Let God: God has a specific calling and purpose for your spouse's work life that may be completely different from your vision. He can open doors that no one can shut and close doors that lead nowhere. The Holy Spirit can give your spouse clarity about their gifts, passion for their calling, and wisdom in career decisions. God can also work through workplace challenges to develop character, create opportunities for ministry, and teach dependence on Him rather than worldly success.

Scripture: *"Commit your work to the Lord, and your plans will be established."* - Proverbs 16:3

Prayer for Your Spouse: *"Lord, I place my spouse's career completely in Your hands. Open the right doors and close the wrong ones. Give them clarity about their calling and passion for the work You've designed them to do. Protect them from workplace stress and toxicity. Use their job as a platform for ministry and character development. Help them find their identity in You, not in worldly success. Guide their career path according to Your perfect plan. Amen."*

Questions for the Heart:

What career dreams or timeline am I imposing on my spouse that may not align with God's calling for their life?

How does my definition of "success" differ from God's, and where am I pushing worldly achievement over spiritual fulfillment?

What fears about financial security or social status drive my need to manage my spouse's career choices?

How can I support my spouse's professional journey without trying to direct or rescue them from workplace challenges?

Prayer for You: *"My dear child, I see how much you want your spouse to succeed and thrive in their work, but your vision of their career path may not match the unique calling I have placed on their life. The dreams you have for them come from love, but they may be limiting the greater purpose I want to fulfill through their work.*

I have gifted your spouse with unique talents, passions, and a calling that only they can fulfill. Sometimes My path for them will look different from what the world calls success. Sometimes I will use seasons of struggle, disappointment, or even seeming failure to prepare them for something greater than you can imagine.

Trust Me with their professional journey. I know when to open doors and when to close them. I know when to promote and when to redirect. I can use a difficult boss to build character, a missed opportunity to redirect their path, or an unexpected job loss to launch them into their true calling.

Your role is to encourage and support, not to manage or rescue. When you step back from trying to control their career, you give Me room to work in ways that will surprise you both. Their greatest professional fulfillment will come when they discover the work I created them to do, not when they achieve the success you envision for them.

Trust My timing and My methods. I am preparing them for something beautiful."

TOGETHERNESS AS A COUPLE

Day 7

Let Go: Stop trying to compete with outside friendships, hobbies, or activities for your spouse's attention. Release the temptation to criticize every interest that doesn't include you or to manufacture guilt about time spent away from the marriage.

Let God: God can work in your spouse's heart to create proper priorities and help them see when outside influences are damaging your relationship. He can convict them about activities or friendships that pull them away from their marriage covenant and inspire them to invest more intentionally in your relationship. The Holy Spirit can give them discernment about influences that don't align with their values and create a genuine desire to build something meaningful with you. God can also open their eyes to see how their choices affect you and motivate them to pursue shared interests and quality time together.

Scripture: *"Two are better than one, because they have a good reward for their toil. For if they fall, one will lift up the other; but woe to one who is alone and falls and does not have another to help." -* Ecclesiastes 4:9-10

Prayer for Your Spouse: *"Lord, help my spouse see the value of investing in our relationship together. If there are friendships or activities that are pulling them away from our marriage, give them discernment to recognize this and wisdom to establish proper boundaries. Create in them a genuine desire to spend quality time with me and build shared experiences. Protect them from influences that would encourage them to neglect our marriage. Help them prioritize our relationship and find joy in doing life together as a team. Amen."*

Questions for the Heart:

What insecurities or fears drive my need to compete with my spouse's friendships and outside interests?

Where am I being possessive rather than loving, and how is this pushing my spouse away instead of drawing them closer?

What legitimate needs for connection and quality time do I have that I can express without guilt-tripping or manipulating?

How can I develop my own interests and friendships so that my spouse isn't carrying the full burden of meeting all my social and emotional needs?

Prayer for You: *"Beloved, your desire for closeness and connection with your spouse is beautiful and natural, but I see how fear and insecurity sometimes turn this longing into possessiveness. You worry that their friendships and interests are taking them away from you, when they might actually be enriching the person they bring back to your marriage.*

I designed marriage to be intimate and close, but not suffocating. Your spouse needs space to be the individual I created them to be, to pursue interests that bring them joy, and to maintain friendships that encourage their growth. When you try to limit these connections out of fear, you often create the very distance you're trying to prevent.

Trust Me with your spouse's heart. If there are friendships or activities that are truly harmful to your marriage, I will convict them and give them wisdom to establish proper boundaries. But many of the things that worry you are actually gifts I'm using to shape them into the person you'll love even more deeply.

Focus on making your time together so rich and enjoyable that they naturally want more of it. Be the kind of person they're excited to come home to. Develop your own interests and friendships so you're not depending on them to meet every emotional need.

When you love with open hands instead of clinched fists, you create space for a love that chooses you freely rather than stays with you out of obligation. That kind of love is worth waiting for."

HEALTH AND HABITS

Day 8

Let Go: Stop nagging about diet, exercise, sleep, or other health choices. Release the burden of being their health monitor or personal trainer.

Let God: God cares deeply about your spouse's physical body as His temple, and He can create motivation for healthy choices from within. The Holy Spirit can convict them about habits that harm their body, inspire them to make better choices, and give them self-control in areas of struggle. God can also use health challenges to draw your spouse closer to Him and teach them to depend on His strength rather than their own.

Scripture: *"Or do you not know that your body is a temple of the Holy Spirit within you, whom you have from God?"* - 1 Corinthians 6:19

Prayer for Your Spouse: *"Lord, help my spouse see their body as Your temple and treat it with respect. Create in them a desire for healthy choices and give them self-control in areas where they struggle. Motivate them to exercise, eat well, and get proper rest. If there are harmful habits, break their power and replace them with life-giving ones. Use their physical health to bring glory to You. Amen."*

Questions for the Heart:

What fears about my spouse's health drive my need to monitor and control their physical choices?

Where has my concern for their wellbeing crossed the line into nagging, criticism, or manipulation?

How do my attempts to be their health coach affect the atmosphere of love and acceptance in our marriage?

What would it look like to support their health goals without taking responsibility for their choices?

Prayer for You: *"My caring child, I see your heart's concern for your spouse's physical wellbeing. You love them deeply and want them to be healthy, strong, and around for many years to come. But your worry has led you to take on a burden that belongs to them and to Me.*

Their body is indeed My temple, and I care about their physical health even more than you do. But lasting change in health habits must come from internal motivation, not external pressure. When you constantly monitor their food choices, exercise habits, or sleep patterns, you often create shame and rebellion rather than the healthy changes you desire.

I can speak to their heart about their body in ways your words never could. I can create genuine desire for healthy choices, give them self-control in areas where they struggle, and motivate them to care for the body I've given them. Sometimes I even use health challenges to draw them closer to Me and teach them dependence on My strength.

Your role is to love them as they are while trusting Me to work in their heart about health choices. Create a home environment that supports healthy living without policing their decisions. Model good choices without preaching about them. Offer encouragement without taking responsibility for their progress.

Love them at every size, in every season of health, and through every stage of their journey. That kind of unconditional love often motivates change more than any amount of nagging ever could."

PAST HURTS AND EMOTIONAL HEALING

Day 9

Let Go: Stop trying to fix their emotional wounds, heal their past hurts, or rush their processing of difficult experiences. Release the need to be their therapist.

Let God: God is the ultimate healer of hearts, and He knows every wound your spouse carries. He can bring healing to the deepest places of pain in ways that human effort never could. The Holy Spirit can comfort them in their grief, give them courage to face difficult memories, and free them from the chains of past trauma. God can turn their pain into purpose and use their healing journey to help others.

Scripture: *"He heals the brokenhearted, and binds up their wounds."* - Psalm 147:3

Prayer for Your Spouse: *"Great Physician, You see every wound in my spouse's heart and every painful memory they carry. Bring Your healing touch to the deepest places of hurt. Comfort them in their pain, give them courage to face difficult truths, and set them free from the chains of the past. Turn their wounds into wisdom and their pain into purpose. Use their healing journey to bring hope to others. Amen."*

Questions for the Heart:

What painful areas of my spouse's past am I trying to heal through my own efforts instead of trusting God's perfect timing?

Where am I being impatient with their emotional healing process and trying to rush them toward wholeness?

How do my attempts to "fix" their emotional wounds sometimes prevent them from processing their pain in healthy ways?

What boundaries do I need to establish so I can support their healing without taking responsibility for their emotional wellbeing?

Prayer for You: *"Tender-hearted one, your desire to heal your spouse's emotional wounds comes from such deep love, but you cannot reach the places in their heart that only I can touch. The pain they carry from their past is real and significant, and it affects your marriage in ways that frustrate and sometimes frighten you.*

But healing from deep wounds is a sacred process that cannot be rushed or managed by human effort. The trauma, abandonment, betrayal, or abuse they experienced created layers of protection and pain that must be carefully and gently unwrapped. This is work that requires My infinite patience and supernatural power.

You cannot love them out of their depression, reason them out of their anxiety, or positive-think them out of their trauma responses. When you try to be their counselor or fix their emotional pain, you often add pressure to an already wounded heart.

I am the Great Physician, and I specialize in healing hearts. I know exactly which memories need to be faced, which lies need to be replaced with truth, and which wounds need My supernatural touch. I will bring the right people, resources, and experiences into their life at the right time to facilitate their healing."

Your job is to provide a safe, loving environment where healing can happen. Be patient with their process. Celebrate small steps forward. Hold space for their pain without trying to eliminate it. Love them in their brokenness while trusting Me to make them whole.

Some of the most beautiful people I know are those I've healed from the deepest wounds. Trust My process."

NEEDS AND EXPECTATIONS

Day 10

Let Go: Stop trying to force your spouse to adopt your values, meet all your needs, or live up to expectations they never agreed to. Release the assumption that they should automatically know and prioritize what matters most to you.

Let God: God can help you and your spouse discover shared values and communicate your needs clearly and lovingly. The Holy Spirit can create understanding between you about what matters most to each of you and help you find ways to honor each other's core values. God can also help you distinguish between legitimate needs and unrealistic expectations, and give you both wisdom about how to love each other well while maintaining your individual identity.

Scripture: *"Do nothing from selfish ambition or conceit, but in humility regard others as better than yourselves."* - Philippians 2:3

Prayer for Your Spouse: *"Lord, help my spouse understand what values and needs are most important to me, and help me understand what matters most to them. Create bridges of understanding between us where we differ and help us find common ground in our shared love for You. Give them a heart that wants to honor what's important to me, and give me grace for areas where we may always be different. Help us both distinguish between needs and wants, and show us how to love each other well. Amen."*

Questions for the Heart:

What values, needs, and expectations do I have that I've never clearly communicated to my spouse?

Where am I expecting my spouse to meet needs that only God can meet, or to automatically know what I've never expressed?

How do I react when my spouse's values or priorities differ from mine, and am I trying to change them instead of understanding them?

What would it look like to share my heart clearly while respecting their right to have different perspectives and priorities?

Prayer for You: *"My dear child, every person brings different values, needs, and expectations into marriage based on their family background, personality, and life experiences. The conflicts you're *experiencing may come from assuming your spouse shares your priorities or should automatically know what matters to you.*

You cannot force someone to value what you value or to meet needs you've never clearly expressed. Your spouse is not a mind reader, and they may genuinely not understand what's most important to you if you haven't communicated it clearly and kindly.

I want to help you both understand each other's heart better. Some of your expectations may be reasonable requests that your spouse would gladly honor if they understood them. Others may be unrealistic hopes that need to be adjusted or met in different ways.

Learn to share your needs and values clearly without demanding that your spouse adopt them as their own. Respect their right to have different priorities while asking them to consider what matters to you. Find ways to honor each other's values even when they differ from your own.

I can create understanding and compromise between you in areas where you differ, and I can help you both distinguish between legitimate needs and unrealistic expectations. Focus on clear, loving communication rather than silent assumptions or demands for change.

Your marriage will be stronger when you both feel heard and understood, even in areas where you may always be different."

PACE OF CHANGE IN YOUR MARRIAGE

Day 11

Let Go: Stop demanding that your marriage improve on your timeline. Release frustration when growth feels slow or setbacks occur.

Let God: God's timing for transformation is perfect, even when it doesn't match your expectations. He knows exactly what needs to happen in your spouse's heart and when they'll be ready for each step of growth. The Holy Spirit can work during seasons that seem stagnant, preparing the ground for breakthrough you can't yet see. God can use the waiting to develop patience in you and deeper transformation in your spouse that wouldn't happen with quick fixes.

Scripture: *"Wait for the Lord; be strong, and let your heart take courage; wait for the Lord!"* - Psalm 27:14

Prayer for Your Spouse: *"Patient God, I place the timing of change in our marriage completely in Your hands. Work in my spouse's heart according to Your perfect schedule, not mine. During seasons that feel slow, continue the deep work that I cannot see. Prepare them for breakthrough in Your timing. Use this waiting period to develop character in both of us that will sustain lasting change. Amen."*

Questions for the Heart:

What expectations do I have about how quickly my marriage should improve, and where do these timelines come from?

How does my impatience with the pace of change create additional pressure and stress in our relationship?

What is God trying to teach me about patience, trust, and His timing during this waiting season?

How can I find contentment and hope in our marriage today while still trusting and looking forward to positive change?

Prayer for You: *"My patient child, I know the waiting is hard. You've been praying and hoping for changes in your marriage, and the slow pace of progress tests your faith and resolve. You wonder if I'm really working, if your spouse will ever change, if your marriage will ever become what you dream it could be. Yet I am at work, even in the waiting. Trust that in My time, your story will unfold with grace and renewal.*

I want you to know that I am never idle, never sleeping, never unconcerned about your marriage. Even in seasons that feel stagnant, I am working beneath the surface, preparing hearts, shifting circumstances, and laying groundwork for breakthroughs you cannot yet see. My timing is perfect, even when it doesn't match your timeline.

Quick fixes and rapid changes rarely produce lasting transformation. The deep work I want to do in your spouse's heart takes time, patience, and the right circumstances. Some changes require them to be ready to receive what I want to give. Other changes require preparation work in both of your hearts that wouldn't happen with instant solutions.

Use this waiting time to grow in your own character. Let Me develop patience, perseverance, and trust in you. Focus on becoming the spouse I'm calling you to be rather than waiting for your spouse to change first. Often, the breakthrough comes when both of you are ready, not just one.

Your marriage story is still being written, and the best chapters may be yet to come. Trust My timing and rest in My love."

RESPONSE TO YOUR LOVE AND AFFECTION

Day 12

Let Go: Stop trying to earn love, manipulate affection, or control how they express feelings. Release expectations about how they should respond to your efforts.

Let God: God can soften your spouse's heart toward you and increase their capacity to both receive and give love. He can heal wounds that make them defensive or distant, remove barriers that prevent intimacy, and create genuine appreciation for your love. The Holy Spirit can work in them to express affection in ways that speak to your heart and help them see you through God's eyes. God's love flowing through them will be far more genuine than anything you could manipulate.

Scripture: *"Above all, clothe yourselves with love, which binds everything together in perfect harmony."* – Colossians 3:14

Prayer for Your Spouse: *"God of love, pour Your love into my spouse's heart so they can love me freely and genuinely. Remove any barriers that prevent intimacy between us. Heal wounds that make them defensive or distant. Help them see me through Your eyes and appreciate the ways I try to show love. Increase their capacity to both receive and express affection. Let Your love flow through them to me. Amen."*

Questions for the Heart:

What expectations do I have about how my spouse should respond to my expressions of love, and how do unmet expectations affect my heart?

Where am I trying to earn or manipulate love instead of giving it freely without conditions?

How do my attempts to control their affection create distance rather than the closeness I desire?

What would it look like to love my spouse without needing them to love me back in specific ways?

Prayer for You: *"Beloved, your heart longs to be loved, cherished, and appreciated by your spouse, and this desire is beautiful and natural. But I see how your need for their love sometimes turns into attempts to control how they express it, when they show it, and how much they demonstrate it.*

Love cannot be forced, earned, or manipulated. The affection you crave must flow freely from their heart, or it will never satisfy the deep longing in your soul. When you try to control their response to your love, you often create pressure that makes genuine expression more difficult for them.

I want to fill your heart so completely with My love that you can love your spouse without needing them to love you back in specific ways. When your identity and security rest in My unchanging love for you, you're free to give love as a gift rather than an investment expecting specific returns.

Trust Me to work in your spouse's heart about their capacity to love and express affection. Some people need healing from past wounds before they can love freely. Others need time to learn how to express love in ways that speak to your heart. Still others need to experience unconditional love before they can give it.

Love them as I have loved you—freely, consistently, without condition or expectation of return. That kind of love creates an environment where their heart can soften and their affection can flow more naturally. Focus on loving well rather than being loved perfectly."

COMMUNICATION AND CONFLICT RESOLUTION

Day 13

Let Go: Stop trying to control how they argue, what words they use, or force them to communicate exactly your way. Release the need to win every disagreement or make them admit you're right.

Let God: God can work in your spouse's heart to create better listening skills, gentler responses during conflict, and wisdom in choosing their words. The Holy Spirit can convict them when they're being harsh, defensive, or unfair, and inspire them to seek understanding rather than just being understood. God can soften their heart during heated moments and give them the humility to apologize when they're wrong. He can also help them see your perspective and communicate their needs without attacking your character.

Scripture: *"Let no evil talk come out of your mouths, but only what is useful for building up, as there is need, so that your words may give grace to those who hear."* - Ephesians 4:29

Prayer for Your Spouse: *"Lord, give my spouse wisdom in how they communicate with me, especially during conflict. Help them choose words that build up rather than tear down. When we disagree, give them a heart that seeks to understand rather than just to be right. Convict them when their words are harsh and inspire them to speak with grace. Help them listen to my heart, not just my words. Make our communication a tool for deeper intimacy, not deeper wounds. Amen."*

Questions for the Heart:

What communication patterns or responses from my spouse trigger my need to correct their approach or control the conversation?

How do my attempts to manage our conflicts actually escalate tension rather than resolve issues?

Where am I more focused on winning arguments than understanding my spouse's heart and perspective?

What would it look like to trust God to convict my spouse about their communication while focusing on my own words and responses?

Prayer for You: *"My dear child, I see how much it hurts when communication with your spouse becomes a battleground instead of a bridge to deeper understanding. You long for conversations that build intimacy rather than create wounds, but your attempts to control how they communicate often make matters worse.*

Communication is a skill that must be learned and a heart issue that must be healed. Your spouse's harsh words, defensive responses, or poor listening skills may stem from past wounds, learned patterns, or simply a lack of understanding about how their communication affects you. These issues take time and My intervention to heal.

You cannot change how your spouse communicates through arguments, corrections, or demands. But I can work in their heart to create gentleness where there was harshness, listening where there was defensiveness, and understanding where there was selfishness. My conviction is far more effective than your criticism.

Focus on being the kind of communicator you want your spouse to be. Speak with grace even when they speak with harshness. Listen to understand even when they seem unwilling to hear you. Respond with love even when they respond with anger. Your example will often teach more than your words.

Trust Me to work in their heart about their communication patterns. Pray for them instead of lecturing them. Love them through their poor communication while believing I can teach them to speak and listen with wisdom.

I am the God who brings understanding out of confusion and peace out of conflict. Trust My ability to transform your conversations."

PHYSICAL INTIMACY

Day 14

Let Go: Stop trying to control the frequency, timing, or initiation of physical intimacy. Release expectations about how affection should be expressed or received.

Let God: God designed marital intimacy as a beautiful expression of oneness, and He can work in your spouse's heart to restore desire, remove barriers, and create genuine connection. The Holy Spirit can heal wounds from the past that affect intimacy, address insecurities that create distance, and inspire them to prioritize physical closeness in your marriage. God can also help them understand your needs and find joy in expressing love through physical affection.

Scripture: *"The husband should give to his wife her conjugal rights, and likewise the wife to her husband."* - 1 Corinthians 7:3

Prayer for Your Spouse: *"Lord, You created physical intimacy as a gift for marriage. Work in my spouse's heart to remove any barriers that prevent closeness between us. Heal past wounds that affect our physical relationship. Help them understand my needs for affection and create in them a genuine desire to connect with me physically. Remove insecurities, fears, or distractions that hinder intimacy. Restore joy and passion to our physical relationship. Amen."*

Questions for the Heart:

What expectations do I have about physical intimacy that may be creating pressure rather than invitation in our relationship?

How do my attempts to control or manipulate physical affection affect the atmosphere of love and safety in our marriage?

What insecurities or fears of my own might be contributing to intimacy challenges in our relationship?

How can I create an environment of emotional safety and unconditional love that naturally encourages physical closeness?

Prayer for You: *"My precious child, I understand the deep longing in your heart for physical intimacy and connection with your spouse. This desire is beautiful and God-given, but your attempts to control or manipulate physical affection often create the opposite of what you're seeking.*

Intimacy cannot be demanded, scheduled, or earned through good behavior or guilt trips. It flows naturally from hearts that feel safe, loved, and connected. When you pressure your spouse for physical affection, you often create anxiety and resistance rather than desire and enthusiasm.

I know this area of your marriage may be causing you pain, loneliness, or frustration. You may wonder if your spouse finds you attractive, if they still love you, or if your physical relationship will ever be what you hope it could be. These concerns are valid, and your heart matters deeply to Me.

Trust Me to work in your spouse's heart about physical intimacy. There may be wounds from the past that need healing, insecurities that need addressing, or simply misunderstandings about your needs that require My gentle conviction. Some barriers to intimacy take time and patience to overcome.

Focus on creating emotional intimacy and safety in your marriage. Often, physical closeness follows emotional connection. Love your spouse unconditionally, not based on their physical response to you. Show affection without always expecting it to lead somewhere. Build trust and emotional intimacy that creates a foundation for physical connection.

I designed intimacy to be a beautiful gift between you. Trust Me to restore what has been broken and to create something even more beautiful than what you've lost."

ADDICTIONS OR DESTRUCTIVE HABITS

Day 15

Let Go: Stop trying to monitor, control, hide, or cure their addictive behaviors through your own efforts. Release the illusion that you can love them out of addiction or manage their recovery.

Let God: God has power to break every chain of addiction, no matter how strong it seems. He can create genuine conviction that leads to repentance, provide supernatural strength to resist temptation, and bring healing to the underlying wounds that fuel addictive behavior. The Holy Spirit can work through various means—professional help, support groups, accountability partners—to bring freedom. God can also give your spouse the humility to admit their need for help and the courage to take necessary steps toward recovery.

Scripture: *"The Lord is near to the brokenhearted, and saves the crushed in spirit."* – Psalm 34:18

Prayer for Your Spouse: *"Lord, You have power to break every chain that binds my spouse. Whatever addiction or destructive habit holds them captive, I pray for Your intervention. Create genuine conviction in their heart and give them the courage to admit their need for help. Provide the right resources, people, and support systems for their recovery. Heal the underlying wounds that fuel this addiction. Give them supernatural strength to resist temptation and hope for complete freedom. Amen."*

Questions for the Heart:

What fears and attempts at control am I using to try to manage my spouse's addiction, and how are these efforts affecting my own wellbeing?

Where am I enabling their destructive behavior by protecting them from consequences or making excuses for their choices?

How has living with addiction affected my ability to trust God with outcomes I cannot control?

What boundaries do I need to establish to protect my own emotional and spiritual health while still loving my spouse?

Prayer for You: *"My hurting child, I see the pain, fear, and exhaustion that comes from loving someone trapped in addiction. You've tried everything you know to do—pleading, threatening, hid-*

ing, monitoring, enabling, and controlling—but the addiction remains stronger than your efforts to defeat it.

You are not responsible for your spouse's addiction, and you cannot cure it through your love, vigilance, or sacrifice. Addiction is a spiritual battle that requires My supernatural intervention. The chains that bind your spouse are too strong for human effort to break, but nothing is too strong for Me.

I know you're afraid of what might happen if you stop trying to manage their behavior. You fear they'll hit bottom, lose everything, or hurt themselves beyond repair. But sometimes hitting bottom is exactly what someone needs to finally look up and cry out for My help.

Your role is not to be their savior—I am their Savior. Your role is to love them while protecting your own heart, to pray for them while maintaining healthy boundaries, and to trust Me with outcomes you cannot control. Sometimes the most loving thing you can do is step back and let them experience the consequences of their choices.

I love your spouse even more than you do, and I have not given up on them. I am working even when you cannot see it, even when they seem to be getting worse. Recovery is possible, healing is available, and freedom is within reach—but it must come through My power, not your efforts.

Trust Me with their addiction. Focus on your own healing and relationship with Me. Let Me be their Deliverer while you learn to be their loving spouse, not their manager."

EMOTIONS AND MENTAL HEALTH

Day 16

Let Go: Stop trying to fix their depression, anxiety, anger, or mood swings through your own efforts. Release the burden of being responsible for their emotional well-being.

Let God: God is the healer of minds and emotions, and He can bring peace to troubled hearts in ways that human effort cannot. The Holy Spirit can comfort them in depression, calm their anxiety, and help them process anger in healthy ways. God can work through professional counselors, medication, lifestyle changes, and His Word to bring emotional healing. He can also give you wisdom about when to encourage professional help and how to be supportive without enabling unhealthy patterns.

Scripture: *"Those of steadfast mind you keep in peace—in peace because they trust in you."* - Isaiah 26:3

Prayer for Your Spouse: *"Prince of Peace, You see my spouse's emotional struggles and mental battles. Bring Your healing touch to their mind and heart. Calm their anxiety, lift their depression, and help them process anger in healthy ways. Show us when professional help is needed and guide us to the right resources. Give them hope in dark moments and peace in troubled times. Help me support them well without trying to fix what only You can heal. Amen."*

Questions for the Heart:

What emotional struggles of my spouse trigger my need to fix, rescue, or take responsibility for their mental health?

How do my attempts to manage their emotions affect both their healing process and my own emotional wellbeing?

Where am I carrying guilt or responsibility for their mental health struggles that belongs to God and professional helpers?

What does healthy support look like versus enabling behavior in our relationship?

Prayer for You: *"Beloved, living with someone who struggles with mental health challenges tests your faith, patience, and endurance in ways that few people understand. You've watched your spouse battle depression, anxiety, or other emotional struggles, and your heart breaks for their pain while you feel helpless to fix it.*

You are not responsible for your spouse's mental health, and you cannot heal their emotional wounds through your love alone. Mental health struggles often have complex roots—chemical imbalances, past trauma, genetic predisposition, or spiritual battles—that require My supernatural healing and often professional intervention.

Your attempts to manage their moods, eliminate their triggers, or create perfect environments to prevent their struggles may actually enable unhealthy patterns rather than promote healing. Your spouse must learn to manage their own mental health with My help and appropriate professional support.

I see how much you love them and want them to be whole. Your compassion and concern reflect My heart for the hurting. But I want to free you from the exhausting burden of trying to be their emotional stabilizer. That's too heavy a load for any human to carry.

Trust Me with their mental health struggles. Encourage them to seek professional help when needed. Support them with love and prayer while maintaining your own emotional health. Set boundaries that protect your wellbeing while still showing compassion for their struggles.

I am the God who heals broken minds and wounded hearts. What seems hopeless to you is not hopeless to Me. Continue to pray, love, and hope while trusting Me with their healing journey."

TECHNOLOGY AND SOCIAL MEDIA BOUNDARIES

Day 17

Let Go: Stop trying to monitor their screen time, control their social media interactions, or manage their online activities. Release the need to police their phone usage during family time or criticize their digital habits. Stop competing with devices for their attention or trying to force technology boundaries through arguments and complaints.

Let God: God can work in your spouse's heart to create healthy boundaries with technology that prioritize real relationships over digital distractions. The Holy Spirit can convict them when screen time is interfering with family connection, when social media interactions are inappropriate, or when digital habits are damaging their relationships. God can help them see how their use of technology affects you and your family, and inspire them to choose presence over pixels. He can also give them discernment about online relationships and activities that don't honor their marriage covenant.

Scripture: *"...training us to renounce impiety and worldly passions, and in the present age to live lives that are self-controlled, upright, and godly."*– Titus 2:12

Prayer for Your Spouse: *"Lord, help my spouse develop healthy boundaries with technology that honor You and our relationship. Convict them when screen time is taking priority over family time or when social media is creating distance between us. Give them wisdom about appropriate online interactions and help them recognize when digital activities are harming our marriage. Create in them a desire to be fully present with me and our family. Help them use technology as a tool rather than allowing it to become a master. Guide them to invest more in real relationships than virtual ones. Amen."*

Questions for the Heart:

What fears drive my need to monitor or control my spouse's technology use, and how do these attempts affect trust in our relationship?

Where am I competing with devices instead of creating an environment where my spouse naturally wants to engage with me?

How has technology affected the intimacy and connection in our marriage, and what is my role in addressing this?

What would it look like to model healthy technology boundaries while trusting God to convict my spouse about their digital habits?

Prayer for You: "*My child, I understand your frustration when technology seems to steal your spouse's attention and create distance in your marriage. The constant pull of phones, social media, and digital entertainment can make you feel like you're competing with a screen for your spouse's heart.*

But your attempts to control or monitor their technology use often create more conflict than connection. Digital boundaries must come from internal conviction, not external pressure. When you try to manage their screen time or police their online activities, you often push them toward secretive behavior rather than open communication.

I can work in their heart far more effectively than your criticism can. I can create conviction about time wasted on meaningless scrolling, inappropriate online interactions, or digital habits that harm your relationship. I can help them see how their technology use affects you and inspire them to choose real presence over virtual distraction.

Focus on making your real-world interactions so engaging and fulfilling that digital alternatives lose their appeal. Create phone-free zones and activities that naturally draw you together. Model the healthy boundaries you want to see rather than demanding them.

I know this battle feels overwhelming because technology is designed to be addictive. Your spouse may not even realize how deeply these digital habits have rewired their brain for constant stimulation and immediate gratification. This is not a character flaw—it's a carefully engineered response that affects millions of people.

But I am more powerful than any algorithm, more compelling than any notification, and more satisfying than any digital experience. I can break through the fog of digital distraction and awaken your spouse to the beauty of real presence, genuine conversation, and authentic intimacy. I can restore their ability to sit quietly, listen deeply, and engage fully with the person right in front of them. The same brain that has been trained to crave digital stimulation can be retrained to crave real connection.

Trust Me to open their eyes to how technology may be interfering with the intimacy I want you to share. I designed marriage for deep connection, and I can help them choose real relationship over digital substitutes. Your faithful love and patient prayers are creating the foundation for this transformation, even when you can't see the progress yet."

FORGIVENESS AND HEALING FROM HURTS

Day 18

Let Go: Stop trying to force apologies, make them understand how deeply they hurt you, or control the timeline for their repentance. Release the need for them to grovel or prove their remorse.

Let God: God can work in your spouse's heart to create genuine conviction about the pain they've caused you. The Holy Spirit can help them see their actions through your eyes and inspire heartfelt repentance that leads to real change. God can soften their heart toward you, remove pride that prevents genuine apology, and create a desire to rebuild trust. He can also work in your own heart to forgive even before they repent, freeing you from bitterness while He works on their heart.

Scripture: *"and be kind to one another, tenderhearted, forgiving one another, as God in Christ has forgiven you."* - Ephesians 4:32

Prayer for Your Spouse: *"Lord, work in my spouse's heart about the ways they have hurt me. Give them eyes to see their actions through my perspective and create genuine conviction that leads to repentance. Remove any pride that prevents them from apologizing sincerely. Help them understand the depth of pain they've caused and inspire them to make real changes, not just say sorry. Give them a heart that wants to rebuild trust and heal our relationship. And help me forgive as You have forgiven me. Amen."*

Questions for the Heart:

What hurts am I holding onto that are preventing me from loving my spouse freely while waiting for God to work in their heart?

How do my attempts to force apologies or prove my pain actually hinder the healing process in our relationship?

Where am I making my forgiveness conditional on their repentance instead of following Christ's example of forgiving first?

What would it look like to release my spouse from the debt of their wrongdoing while still hoping for genuine repentance?

Prayer for You: *"My wounded child, I see the deep hurts you carry from your spouse's actions, words, or neglect. The pain is real, the wounds are significant, and your longing for acknowledgment and repentance is understandable. You want them to see how much they've hurt you and to make it right.*

But your attempts to force understanding or manufacture genuine repentance often create defensiveness rather than conviction. True sorrow for sin and genuine repentance must come from My work in their heart, not from your explanations of your pain.

I want to free you from the prison of unforgiveness while I work on their heart about repentance. Forgiveness doesn't mean excusing their behavior or pretending it didn't hurt. It means releasing them from the debt they owe you and trusting Me to deal with their heart about the pain they've caused.

When you forgive before they repent, you're following My example. I forgave you while you were still My enemy. I loved you before you loved Me back. This kind of forgiveness doesn't enable their bad behavior—it frees your heart from bitterness while creating space for genuine conviction to work.

Trust Me to bring them to genuine repentance in My timing. My conviction is far more powerful than your hurt feelings in creating real change. Focus on keeping your own heart free from bitterness while believing that I can create genuine sorrow and repentance in them.

Forgiveness is not weakness—it's the strongest thing you can do. It breaks the power of their sin over your heart while positioning them to receive My conviction about their need to repent."

TEMPTATIONS AND FIDELITY

Day 19

Let Go: Stop trying to monitor their every move, check their phone, or control their environment to prevent temptation. Release the exhausting burden of being their accountability system.

Let God: God can strengthen your spouse against temptation and create genuine integrity that comes from the heart, not external pressure. The Holy Spirit can convict them about inappropriate relationships, lustful thoughts, or situations that compromise their faithfulness. God can remove the appeal of temptation and create a deep love for you that makes fidelity natural rather than forced. He can also surround them with accountability and remove people or circumstances that lead them astray.

Scripture: *"No testing has overtaken you that is not common to everyone. God is faithful, and he will not let you be tested beyond your strength, but with the testing he will also provide the way out so that you may be able to endure it."* - 1 Corinthians 10:13

Prayer for Your Spouse: *"Lord, protect my spouse from temptations that would damage our marriage. Give them strength to resist inappropriate relationships and lustful thoughts. Create in them a heart that is fully devoted to me and finds complete satisfaction in our relationship. Surround them with accountability and remove influences that lead them toward unfaithfulness. When temptation comes, provide a way of escape and remind them of their covenant with me. Amen."*

Questions for the Heart:

What fears about my spouse's faithfulness are driving my need to monitor and control their interactions and environment?

How do my attempts at surveillance and control affect the trust and intimacy in our marriage?

Where am I trying to be their conscience instead of trusting the Holy Spirit to convict them about inappropriate behavior?

What would it look like to create an atmosphere of love and satisfaction in our marriage that naturally reduces the appeal of outside temptations?

Prayer for You: *"Beloved, I understand the fear that grips your heart when you worry about your spouse's faithfulness. Whether* *you've experienced betrayal before or simply fear the possibility, the temptation to monitor and control their every interaction comes from a place of deep vulnerability.*

But your attempts to be their accountability system often create the very distance and resentment that can make temptation more appealing. When trust is replaced with surveillance, intimacy suffers, and your marriage becomes a prison rather than a sanctuary.

I am far more effective at protecting your marriage than any monitoring system you could create. I can convict your spouse about inappropriate thoughts before they become actions. I can remove tempting people and situations from their path. I can create such satisfaction and joy in your marriage that outside attractions lose their appeal.

Your role is to be the kind of spouse they don't want to betray—loving, attractive, supportive, and enjoyable to be around. Create a marriage so fulfilling that temptations pale in comparison. Trust rather than suspicion, love rather than fear, and intimacy rather than distance are your best protections against infidelity.

If there are real reasons for concern, trust Me to expose what needs to be revealed and to give you wisdom about how to respond. But don't let fear steal the joy and intimacy from your marriage. I am watching over your relationship with eyes that never sleep and love that never fails.

Trust Me to guard your spouse's heart and protect your marriage covenant."

LIFE PURPOSE AND CALLING

Day 20

Let Go: Stop trying to define their purpose or push them toward your vision of what their life should accomplish. Release anxiety about whether they're "living up to their potential."

Let God: God has a unique calling and purpose for your spouse that only He fully understands. The Holy Spirit can reveal their gifts, clarify their mission, and create passion for the work God has designed them to do. God can open doors that align with their purpose and close doors that lead away from it. He can use seasons of confusion or wandering to prepare them for their ultimate calling and give them patience during times of waiting.

Scripture: *"For we are what he has made, created in Christ Jesus for good works, which God prepared beforehand to be our way of life."* - Ephesians 2:10

Prayer for Your Spouse: *"Creator God, reveal to my spouse the unique purpose for which You created them. Clarify their calling and give them passion for the work You've designed them to do. Open doors that align with Your plan and close doors that lead away from it. Help them discover and use their gifts for Your glory. Give them patience during seasons of waiting and confidence in Your timing. Use their life to make a significant impact for Your kingdom. Amen."*

Questions for the Heart:

What dreams and expectations do I have for my spouse's life purpose that may not align with God's calling for them?

How does my anxiety about their "potential" create pressure that hinders their ability to hear God's direction?

Where am I judging their worth by worldly standards of success rather than by God's definition of meaningful impact?

What would it look like to encourage and support their journey of discovering purpose without trying to direct it?

Prayer for You: *"My dear child, I see how much you believe in your spouse and want their life to matter. Your desire for them to discover and fulfill their purpose comes from love, but your attempts to define or direct their calling may actually interfere with the unique work I want to do through them.*

I have plans for your spouse that are far greater and more specific than you can imagine. Their calling may look different from what you envision. Their path to purpose may involve detours, delays, or directions that don't make sense to you. But every step is preparing them for the work I've designed specifically for them.

Some people discover their purpose early and pursue it with passion. Others wander through seasons of uncertainty, trying different paths before finding their true calling. Still others find that their purpose emerges gradually from their current circumstances and experiences. Trust My timing and methods for your spouse.

Your role is to encourage, support, and believe in them without trying to manage their journey. Celebrate their gifts without demanding they use them in ways you think best. Support their dreams without imposing your own. Trust that I am guiding them even when their path seems unclear.

Sometimes the greatest purpose is found in faithfulness in small things. Sometimes significance comes through influence that's never recognized publicly. Sometimes the calling is simply to love well, serve faithfully, and point others to Me through their character and consistency.

Trust Me with their purpose. Your spouse was created for something unique and beautiful, and I will not let their life be wasted. Be patient with the process and believe in the outcome."

TRIALS AND CHALLENGES

Day 21

Let Go: Stop trying to rescue them from every difficulty or solve their problems for them. Release the need to shield them from consequences or smooth every rough path.

Let God: God can use trials to develop character, strengthen faith, and prepare your spouse for greater things. The Holy Spirit can give them wisdom to navigate challenges, courage to face difficulties, and perseverance to endure hardship. God can turn setbacks into setups for breakthrough and use painful experiences to create compassion for others. He knows exactly which trials will produce the character qualities your spouse needs.

Scripture: *"My brothers and sisters, whenever you face trials of any kind, consider it nothing but joy, because you know that the testing of your faith produces endurance."* - James 1:2-3

Prayer for Your Spouse: *"Lord, I place my spouse's trials and challenges in Your hands. Use these difficulties to develop their character and strengthen their faith. Give them wisdom to navigate tough situations and courage to face challenges head-on. Help them see Your purpose in their struggles and trust Your plan even when the path is difficult. Bring good from every setback and use their trials to prepare them for greater things. Amen."*

Questions for the Heart:

What difficulties is my spouse facing that I'm trying to fix or eliminate instead of trusting God to use for their growth?

How does my need to rescue them from challenges prevent them from developing their own strength and resilience?

Where am I more concerned with their comfort than with their character development?

What would it look like to support them through trials while allowing God to use those experiences for their good?

Prayer for You: *"My compassionate child, it's hard to watch someone you love struggle through difficulties, face challenges, or endure pain. Your instinct is to rescue, fix, and smooth their path because you care so deeply about their wellbeing. But your attempts to shield them from every trial may actually interfere with the important work I want to do in their life.*

I allow trials not because I'm uncaring, but because I love your spouse enough to develop their character even when it's uncomfortable. Some of their greatest strengths will be forged in the fire of difficulty. Some of their most important lessons will be learned through challenges they must face themselves.

When you rush in to rescue them from every consequence, solve every problem, or eliminate every difficulty, you rob them of opportunities to grow in strength, wisdom, and faith. They need to learn that they can face hard things and overcome them with My help.

Your role is to be a source of encouragement, prayer, and emotional support—not to be their rescuer from every trial. Walk alongside them through difficulties without trying to carry them through. Believe in their ability to overcome with My strength while offering comfort and hope.

I am using every trial in your spouse's life for good, even when the purpose isn't clear in the moment. Trust My process even when it's painful to watch. Some of the most beautiful people I know are those who have been refined through difficulty and emerged stronger, wiser, and more compassionate.

Support them without rescuing them. Love them through the trials without eliminating them. Trust that I am using every challenge to shape them into the person I created them to be."

INTEGRITY AND REPUTATION

Day 22

Let Go: Stop trying to manage their reputation or control how others perceive them. Release the need to defend them or make excuses for their choices.

Let God: God can work in your spouse's heart to create genuine integrity that cares more about character than image. The Holy Spirit can convict them about areas where their private life doesn't match their public persona and inspire them to live authentically. God can restore damaged reputation through genuine change and protect their name when they're falsely accused. He can also help them value God's approval above human opinion.

Scripture: *"A good name is to be chosen rather than great riches, and favor is better than silver or gold."* - Proverbs 22:1

Prayer for Your Spouse: *"Lord, create genuine integrity in my spouse that cares more about character than reputation. Convict them about any areas where their private life doesn't match their public image. Help them live authentically and value Your approval above human opinion. Restore any damaged reputation through real change in their heart. Protect their name from false accusations and help them build a legacy of honor. Amen."*

Questions for the Heart:

What aspects of my spouse's reputation or public image am I trying to protect that they should be responsible for themselves?

How do my attempts to manage others' perceptions of my spouse affect my own integrity and authenticity?

Where am I making excuses for their behavior instead of allowing them to face the natural consequences of their choices?

What would it look like to support my spouse while allowing them to take ownership of their own character and reputation?

Prayer for You: *"Beloved, I understand how much it matters to you that your spouse is well-regarded and respected by others. When their choices, attitudes, or behavior damage their reputation, you feel the pain as if it were your own. Your desire to protect their image and defend their character comes from love and loyalty.*

But your attempts to manage how others perceive your spouse often prevent them from taking ownership of their own character and the consequences of their choices. When you make excuses for their behav-

ior or try to control others' opinions, you rob them of opportunities to grow in integrity and authenticity.

True integrity must come from within. It cannot be manufactured, managed, or maintained by external efforts. Your spouse must care about their character more than their image, and they must value My approval above human opinion. This transformation can only happen through My work in their heart.

If their reputation has been damaged by their own choices, trust Me to either restore it through genuine change or protect them from unfair judgment. If they're being falsely accused, I can defend them better than you can. If they need to face consequences for their actions, allow those consequences to do their teaching work.

Focus on your own integrity rather than managing theirs. Be the person of character you want them to be. Your authentic life will often inspire them more than your attempts to manage their image ever could.

A reputation built on truth and genuine character will stand the test of time. Trust Me to work in their heart about the importance of living with integrity, and release the burden of protecting their image."

ATTITUDE AND OUTLOOK

Day 23

Let Go: Stop trying to change their perspective through arguments or constant correction. Release the need to fix their negative thinking or pessimistic outlook.

Let God: God can transform your spouse's heart and mind, creating gratitude where there was complaining and hope where there was despair. The Holy Spirit can renew their thinking, help them see situations from God's perspective, and replace negative thought patterns with truth. God can heal wounds that create cynicism and restore joy that makes them pleasant to be around.

Scripture: *"Do not be conformed to this world, but be transformed by the renewing of your minds."* - Romans 12:2

Prayer for Your Spouse: *"Lord, transform my spouse's heart and mind. Replace negative thinking with gratitude, despair with hope, and cynicism with faith. Help them see situations from Your perspective and choose joy even in difficult circumstances. Heal wounds that create bitterness and renew their thinking according to Your truth. Make them a person who brings light and encouragement to others. Amen."*

Questions for the Heart:

What negative attitudes or pessimistic patterns in my spouse trigger my need to correct or fix their perspective?

How do my attempts to change their outlook affect the emotional atmosphere of our relationship?

Where might my spouse's negativity be reflecting deeper wounds or disappointments that need healing rather than correction?

What would it look like to model the positive attitude I want to see while trusting God to transform their thinking?

Prayer for You: *"My dear child, living with someone who consistently sees the negative side of situations, complains frequently, or approaches life with pessimism can drain your joy and test your patience. You want your spouse to be more positive, grateful, and hopeful, but your attempts to correct their attitude often make them more defensive and negative.*

Negative thinking patterns are often rooted in past hurts, disappointments, or learned responses to life's difficulties. Your spouse may be protecting themselves from further disappointment by expecting the worst. These patterns require My healing touch, not your constant corrections.

I can transform your spouse's mind and heart in ways your arguments never could. I can heal the wounds that create cynicism, restore hope where there's been repeated disappointment, and create gratitude where there's been bitterness. My truth can replace the lies that fuel negative thinking.

Your role is to be a source of light and encouragement without trying to force positivity on them. Model the joy and hope you want to see. Speak words of faith and gratitude even when they speak words of doubt and complaint. Create an atmosphere of positivity through your own attitude rather than demanding it from them.

Sometimes the most loving thing you can do is listen to their negative feelings without trying to fix them. Let them process their disappointments and fears while you pray for My healing in their heart. Your acceptance of their struggles while maintaining your own hope will often minister more than your corrections.

Trust Me to renew their mind and restore their joy. Focus on guarding your own heart from their negativity while believing that I can create a grateful, hopeful spirit in them."

ANGER AND FRUSTRATION

Day 24

Let Go: Stop walking on eggshells to avoid their anger or trying to manage their emotional outbursts. Release the fear of their reactions and the responsibility for their emotional regulation.

Let God: God can work in your spouse's heart to heal the roots of anger and create self-control in moments of frustration. The Holy Spirit can convict them about how their anger affects others and teach them healthy ways to process difficult emotions. God can replace quick temper with patience and explosive reactions with gentle responses. He can also reveal underlying hurt or fear that fuels their anger.

Scripture: *"You must understand this, my beloved: let everyone be quick to listen, slow to speak, slow to anger."* – James 1:19

Prayer for Your Spouse: *"Lord, work in my spouse's heart to heal the roots of anger and frustration. Teach them healthy ways to process difficult emotions and give them self-control in moments of temptation to explode. Replace their quick temper with patience and harsh words with gentle responses. Reveal any underlying hurt or fear that fuels their anger. Help them see how their reactions affect our family. Amen."*

Questions for the Heart:

How has my spouse's anger affected my behavior and am I responding with healthy boundaries?

What am I doing to enable or escalate their angry responses instead of creating a calm environment?

How can I protect my own emotional wellbeing while still loving my spouse through their anger struggles?

What would it look like to respond to their anger with grace while not accepting abusive or destructive behavior?

Prayer for You: *"My child, living with someone who struggles with anger is exhausting and frightening. You find yourself treading lightly, trying to avoid triggers, or managing situations to prevent explosive reactions. The unpredictability of their temper has affected your peace and maybe even your sense of safety.*

You are not responsible for managing your spouse's emotional responses, and you cannot heal their anger through your careful behavior. Their anger is their responsibility to address, and it often stems from deeper issues like past hurts, unresolved pain, or learned patterns that require My healing intervention.

I want to free you from the fear of their reactions while also protecting you from any harm their anger might cause. You can love someone struggling with anger while still maintaining boundaries that protect your emotional and physical safety. Love doesn't require you to accept abuse or destructive behavior.

Trust Me to work in their heart about their anger issues. I can reveal the underlying hurt or fear that fuels their explosive reactions. I can teach them healthy ways to process frustration and give them self-control in moments of temptation. My conviction about their anger will be more effective than your fear of it.

Respond to their anger with calm strength rather than fear or retaliation. Don't enable their bad behavior nor escalate conflicts with your own anger either. Model the emotional regulation you want to see while trusting Me to work in their heart.

If their anger becomes dangerous or abusive, seek help and protection. I never want you to endure harm in the name of love. Trust Me to work on their heart while you take care of your own safety and wellbeing."

RELATIONSHIP WITH GOD

Day 25

Let Go: Stop trying to be their spiritual conscience or monitor their obedience to God's commands. Release the pressure to enforce their relationship with Christ.

Let God: God can create a genuine desire in your spouse's heart to obey Him out of love, not obligation. The Holy Spirit can convict them about areas of disobedience and give them strength to follow God's commands. God can make the path of obedience attractive to your spouse and help them understand that following God's ways leads to blessing, not restriction. He can also give them courage to obey even when it's difficult.

Scripture: *"You shall love the Lord your God with all your heart, and with all your soul, and with all your might."* – Deuteronomy 6:5

Prayer for Your Spouse: *"Lord, create in my spouse a heart that wants to obey You out of love, not obligation. Convict them gently about areas of disobedience and give them strength to follow Your commands. Help them see that Your ways lead to life and blessing. Give them courage to obey even when it's difficult or unpopular. Make Your will attractive to them and Your path their greatest desire. Amen."*

Questions for the Heart:

Where am I trying to be my spouse's spiritual police officer instead of trusting the Holy Spirit to convict them about areas of disobedience?

How do my attempts to monitor or enforce their obedience to God affect our relationship and their spiritual journey?

What areas of obedience am I most concerned about in my spouse's life, and what fears drive this concern?

How can I model authentic obedience to God while trusting Him to work in my spouse's heart about their own relationship with Him?

Prayer for You: *"Beloved, your concern for your spouse's obedience to Me reveals a heart that wants them to experience the blessing and protection that comes from walking in My ways. But your attempts to monitor, correct, or enforce their spiritual choices often create resistance rather than the genuine heart change you desire.*

True obedience cannot be forced, managed, or created through external pressure. It must flow from a heart that loves Me and understands that My commands are given for their good, not to restrict their freedom. This kind of heart transformation can only come through My Spirit's work, not through your spiritual supervision.

When you try to be their conscience about spiritual matters, you often take the place of My Holy Spirit, who is far more effective at creating conviction and inspiring obedience. Your corrections may actually harden their heart against the very things you want them to embrace.

Trust Me to work in their heart about areas of disobedience. I know exactly how to create genuine desire for holiness, real sorrow for sin, and authentic hunger for righteousness. My conviction leads to lasting change, while human pressure often leads to rebellion or mere external compliance.

Your role is to live in obedience yourself, demonstrating the joy and peace that comes from following My ways. Let your authentic relationship with Me inspire them rather than your lectures about their relationship with Me. Pray for them instead of preaching to them.

I love your spouse even more than you do, and I desire their obedience more than you can imagine. Trust Me to draw them into willing submission to My will through My love, not through your management."

PAST MISTAKES

Day 26

Let Go: Stop rehearsing your spouse's past failures or holding their mistakes over them like a weapon. Release your grip on old wounds, disappointments, and memories of how they hurt you. Stop defining them by who they were instead of who they're becoming. Let go of the bitter satisfaction that comes from reminding them of their worst moments.

Let God: I finish what I begin. When I start a work of transformation in your spouse's heart, I do not abandon it halfway through or decide their past makes them beyond redemption. The same grace that has covered your mistakes extends to theirs. I have plans for your spouse's future that are not limited by their past failures. I can take the broken pieces of yesterday and build something beautiful for tomorrow. I specialize in new beginnings, fresh starts, and resurrection stories. What looks like wasted years to you is a preparation in My hands. I can redirect the consequences of their past mistakes into wisdom for their future. I can heal what was broken and restore what was lost. Their history does not determine their destiny—I do.

Scripture: *"For I know the plans I have for you, says the Lord, plans for your welfare and not for harm, to give you a future with hope."* - Jeremiah 29:11

Prayer for Your Spouse: *"Lord, help my spouse break free from the chains of their past. Release them from guilt, shame, and regret that keeps them looking backward instead of forward. Give them the courage to accept Your forgiveness and move into the future You have planned for them. Help them see themselves not as defined by their worst moments, but as becoming the person You created them to be. Plant new dreams in their heart that reflect Your redemptive purposes. Give them hope for what lies ahead and freedom from what lies behind. Transform their past pain into future wisdom, their failures into testimonies of Your grace. Amen."*

Questions for My Heart:

What past mistakes of my spouse do I keep bringing up, either aloud or in my mind, instead of truly forgiving and releasing them?

How does my refusal to let go of the past prevent both of us from moving forward into the future God has for our marriage?

Where am I defining my spouse by their worst moments instead of believing in their capacity to change and grow?

What would it look like to genuinely release the past and partner with God in creating a new future together?

Prayer for You: *"My beloved child, I see how tightly you're gripping the past—both your spouse's mistakes and your own. You replay the betrayals, rehearse the disappointments, and catalog every failure as evidence that your marriage is beyond repair. But I am the God of resurrection, and nothing is beyond My ability to redeem.*

The past you keep revisiting is not the future I have planned for your marriage. Yes, painful things happened. Yes, trust was broken. Yes, words were spoken that can't be unsaid and actions were taken that left scars. But I specialize in making all things new, and that includes marriages that look hopelessly broken.

When you constantly remind your spouse of their past failures, you're acting as their accuser, not their redeemer. That's the enemy's job, not yours. I have already covered their sins with My blood—the same blood that covers yours. Who are you to keep uncovering what I have chosen to forgive?

Your spouse needs you to be a partner in hope, not a curator of their failure museum. They need you to believe in who they're becoming, not to constantly remind them of who they were. Every time you bring up the past, you're building a wall between you instead of a bridge toward the future.

I know it's hard to let go when you've been deeply hurt. I know forgiveness feels like letting them off the hook, like saying what they did was acceptable. But forgiveness is not about excusing their behavior—it's about freeing yourself from the prison of bitterness and giving Me room to work in both of your hearts.

The plans I have for your marriage are not determined by your past but by My purposes. I can take the most broken relationships and rebuild them into testimonies of grace. I can transform your deepest wounds into your greatest strengths. I can use the very things that nearly destroyed you to create a marriage more beautiful than what you had before the pain.

But I cannot do this while you're holding onto the past with both hands. You must release what was in order to receive what will be. You must stop looking backward in order to move forward. You must choose to believe that redemption is possible, that change is real, and that I am faithful to complete the good work I have begun.

Trust Me enough to let go of yesterday so you can embrace tomorrow. Your spouse's past does not have to be your marriage's future."

SELF-WORTH AND IDENTITY

Day 27

Let Go: Stop trying to build their self-esteem through constant affirmation or fix their insecurities. Release the burden of being their source of validation.

Let God: God can reveal your spouse's true identity as a beloved child of God and help them find their worth in Christ, not in performance or others' opinions. The Holy Spirit can heal wounds that create insecurity and replace lies with truth about who they are. God can give them confidence that comes from knowing they are fearfully and wonderfully made and deeply loved by their Creator.

Scripture: *"See what love the Father has given us, that we should be called children of God; and that is what we are."* - 1 John 3:1

Prayer for Your Spouse: *"Father, reveal to my spouse their true identity as Your beloved child. Help them find their worth in You, not in performance or others' opinions. Heal wounds that create insecurity and replace lies with truth about who they are in Christ. Give them confidence that comes from knowing they are fearfully and wonderfully made. Help them see themselves as You see them. Amen."*

Questions for the Heart:

How am I trying to build my spouse's self-worth in ways that make me their source of validation rather than pointing them to God?

What insecurities in my spouse trigger my need to constantly affirm or fix their self-image?

Where might my efforts to boost their confidence actually enable unhealthy dependence on external validation?

How can I love and encourage my spouse while trusting God to establish their identity and worth?

Prayer for You: *"Beloved, it breaks your heart to see your spouse struggle with insecurity, self-doubt, or a poor self-image. You want them to know how wonderful, talented, and lovable they are, so you try to build them up through constant affirmation and encouragement. Your heart is beautiful, but your efforts alone cannot heal their wounded sense of worth.*

Insecurity and poor self-image usually stem from deep wounds, past rejections, or lies they've believed about themselves. These issues re-

quire My healing touch and the revelation of their true identity in Me. Your affirmations, while well-meaning, cannot replace the foundational healing only I can provide.

When you try to be their primary source of validation, you may actually reinforce their dependence on external approval rather than helping them find their worth in Me. True confidence must be rooted in My unchanging love and their identity as My child, not in human opinions that can shift and change.

I want to heal your spouse's insecurities at their root and establish their identity on the solid foundation of My love. I can replace the lies they believe about themselves with truth about who they are in Christ. I can heal old wounds that created shame and give them confidence that comes from knowing they are deeply loved and perfectly accepted.

Love them well without trying to fix their self-image. Encourage them without taking responsibility for their confidence. Point them to Me as their source of worth rather than trying to be their source of validation yourself.

Trust Me to show them who they really are and how much they matter. Their security will be unshakeable when it's built on My love rather than human affirmation."

ROLE IN THE HOME

Day 28

Let Go: Stop trying to force them into your vision of what their role should be or criticizing how they contribute to your household. Release expectations about how they should function in your family dynamic.

Let God: God can help your spouse discover their unique role and contribution to your family. The Holy Spirit can give them wisdom about how to best serve your household, whether through providing, nurturing, managing, or supporting in ways that fit their gifts and your family's needs. God can create in them a servant's heart that looks for ways to strengthen your family unit and fulfill their part in making your home a place of peace and love.

Scripture: *"but as for me and my household, we will serve the Lord."* - Joshua 24:15

Prayer for Your Spouse: *"Lord, help my spouse discover their unique role and contribution to our family. Give them wisdom about how to best serve our household according to their gifts and our needs. Create in them a servant's heart that seeks to strengthen our family unit. Help them understand how important their contribution is to making our home a place of peace and love. Guide them in fulfilling their part in serving You through our family. Amen."*

Questions for the Heart:

What expectations do I have about my spouse's role in our family that may not align with their gifts, abilities, or calling?

How do I try to control or criticize their contributions instead of appreciating their unique strengths?

Where am I comparing our family dynamic to others instead of trusting God to show us how to function best together?

What would it look like to celebrate my spouse's unique contributions while trusting God to develop their heart for serving our family?

Prayer for You: *"My dear child, I see how much you care about your family and want every member to contribute to making your home a place of love, peace, and godliness. But your attempts to force your spouse into a specific role or criticize their contributions often create tension rather than the harmony you desire.*

Every family is unique, and every person has different gifts, strengths, and ways of serving. Your spouse may contribute to your family in ways that don't match traditional expectations or your vision of how things should work. Their role may look different from what you see in other families or what you experienced growing up.

I want to show your spouse how to best serve your family according to their gifts and your specific needs. They may be called to contribute through emotional support, practical help, financial provision, spiritual leadership, or creative solutions in ways you haven't considered. Trust Me to develop their heart for serving your family unit.

Instead of criticizing what they don't do, celebrate what they do contribute. Instead of forcing them into a role that doesn't fit, help them discover how their unique gifts can bless your family. Create an atmosphere of appreciation and teamwork rather than criticism and competition.

Your family will function best when each person operates in their strengths while supporting others in their areas of weakness. Trust Me to show both of you how to work together as a team that honors Me and serves your family's needs.

Focus on fulfilling your own role excellently while believing that I can develop your spouse's heart to serve your family in the ways that matter most."

TRUST AND TRUSTWORTHINESS

Day 29

Let Go: Stop trying to force trust through surveillance, testing, or constant reminders of past failures. Release the need to control their trustworthiness through monitoring or manipulation.

Let God: God can work in your spouse's heart to create genuine integrity and reliability that flows from their character, not from external pressure. The Holy Spirit can convict them about areas where they've been untrustworthy and inspire them to rebuild trust through consistent, honest actions over time. God can heal whatever wounds or fears drive untrustworthy behavior and create in them a deep desire to be someone you can depend on completely.

Scripture: *"Whoever is faithful in a very little is faithful also in much; and whoever is dishonest in a very little is dishonest also in much."* - Luke 16:10

Prayer for Your Spouse: *"Lord, work in my spouse's heart to create genuine trustworthiness that comes from their love for You and for me. Convict them about any areas where they've been unreliable or dishonest. Give them the courage to face past failures and the commitment to rebuild trust through consistent actions. Help them understand how precious trust is in our marriage and motivate them to protect it carefully. Make them someone I can depend on completely. Amen."*

Questions for the Heart:

What past betrayals or disappointments make it difficult for me to trust my spouse, and how can I heal from these wounds while still protecting my heart wisely?

Where am I confusing trust with control, and how do my attempts to monitor their trustworthiness actually damage the foundation I'm trying to build?

How has broken trust affected my ability to be vulnerable and intimate in our marriage?

What would it look like to create opportunities for my spouse to demonstrate trustworthiness while protecting myself from further harm?

Prayer for You: *"My wounded child, I see how broken trust has* *affected your heart and your marriage. The pain of betrayal runs deep, and your hesitation to trust again is understandable and wise. You long for a spouse you can depend on completely, but your attempts to force trustworthiness through surveillance often create more distance than security.*

Trust cannot be demanded or manufactured—it must be earned through consistent, reliable actions over time. Your spouse must choose trustworthiness because they value your relationship and their integrity, not because you're monitoring their every move.

I know it's frightening to make yourself vulnerable again after being hurt. But hiding behind walls of suspicion will prevent the intimacy you both need. I can heal your wounded heart while giving you wisdom about how to rebuild trust safely and gradually.

I can work in your spouse's heart far more effectively than your surveillance can. I can create genuine conviction about their need to be trustworthy and give them strength to choose integrity even when it's difficult. Trust Me to work while you focus on healing and creating opportunities for them to prove their reliability.

Healing takes time, and rebuilding trust is a process. Be patient with yourself and with them while I do the deep work that creates lasting change. The trust you rebuild on My foundation will be stronger than what was broken."

LEGACY AND IMPACT

Day 30

Let Go: Stop worrying about whether their life will matter or trying to create significance for them. Release anxiety about their lasting impact.

Let God: God can use your spouse's life to make an eternal impact that may not be visible until heaven. The Holy Spirit can work through their influence on family, friends, coworkers, and community in ways they may never know. God can multiply their small acts of faithfulness and use their testimony to draw others to Christ. He can create a legacy that extends far beyond their lifetime through the lives they touch.

Scripture: *"So let us not grow weary in doing what is right, for we will reap at harvest time, if we do not give up."* - Galatians 6:9

Prayer for Your Spouse: *"Lord, use my spouse's life to make an eternal impact for Your kingdom. Work through their influence* *on family, friends, and community in ways they may never see. Multiply their faithful efforts and use their testimony to draw others to You. Help them invest in things that matter for eternity. Create a legacy through their life that brings glory to Your name and blessing to future generations. Amen."*

Questions for the Heart:

What concerns do I have about my spouse's significance or impact that reflect my own definitions of success rather than God's?

How do my worries about their legacy create pressure that hinders their natural ability to influence others positively?

Where am I trying to create meaning for their life instead of trusting God to use them according to His purposes?

What would it look like to celebrate the ways God is already using my spouse while trusting Him for their ultimate impact?

Prayer for You: *"My precious child, as you complete this thirty-day journey, I want you to know how proud I am of the growth I've seen in your heart. You've learned to release control and trust Me with your spouse in ways that seemed impossible when you began. This final day reminds you to trust Me with something even bigger—your spouse's eternal significance and lasting impact.*

You worry sometimes that their life won't matter, that they're not living up to their potential, or that they won't leave the legacy you hope for them. But I want you to know that I never waste a life surrendered to Me. Every person I create has a unique purpose and potential for impact that extends far beyond what human eyes can see.

Your spouse's significance doesn't depend on their achievements, recognition, or visible success. Some of the most important work in My kingdom happens quietly, behind the scenes, through simple faithfulness and loving relationships. A parent's influence on their children, a friend's encouragement during difficult times, a coworker's consistent kindness—these seemingly small acts often have eternal consequences.

Trust Me to use your spouse's life in ways that may not be recognized until heaven. I can multiply their smallest acts of love, use their testimony to touch hearts they'll never know about, and create ripple effects through their influence that continue for generations.

Stop trying to create significance for them and start celebrating the ways I'm already using them. Their legacy is in My hands, and I promise it will be far greater than either of you can imagine.

Your marriage journey continues, but now you know the secret: when you let go and let Me work, miracles happen in ways that will amaze you."

YOUR NEW WAY OF LOVING

In the Days Ahead

You have walked a journey these past thirty days that few are willing to take. You have discovered that the most powerful thing you can do for your marriage is often the hardest thing to do: nothing. Nothing except pray. Nothing except trust. Nothing except release the person you love most into the hands of the One who loves them even more.

As you close this book, you are not the same person who opened it thirty days ago. You have learned that true love doesn't grasp—it releases. It doesn't control—it covers. It doesn't demand—it trusts. You have discovered that when you step back from trying to be your spouse's Holy Spirit, you create space for the real Holy Spirit to work miracles you never could have orchestrated.

But this is not the end of your journey. It's the beginning of a new way of loving that reflects the heart of God Himself. You have learned to love like Jesus loves—with open hands instead of clenched fists, with prayers instead of demands, with trust instead of control.

Now, as you continue forward, hear these words as if Jesus Himself is speaking them directly to your heart:

MY BELOVED, HERE IS HOW I WANT YOU TO LOVE YOUR SPOUSE:

Love by listening without correcting, for in your silence, I can speak to their heart. *"Let us therefore no longer pass judgment on one another, but resolve instead never to put a stumbling block or hindrance in the way of another."* - Romans 14:13

Love by serving without keeping score, for My love is not a transaction but a gift. *"For you were called to freedom, brothers and sisters; only do not use your freedom as an opportunity for self-indulgence, but through love become slaves to one another."* - Galatians 5:13

Love by encouraging without manipulating, for true encouragement comes from My Spirit, not your agenda. *"Theref ore encourage one another and build up each other, as indeed you are doing."* - 1 Thessalonians 5:11

Love by forgiving without conditions, for I have forgiven you while you were still My enemy. *"Bear with one another and, if* anyone has a complaint against another, forgive each other; just as the Lord has forgiven you, so you also must forgive." Colossians 3:13

Love by praying without ceasing, for this is where your real power lies. *"pray without ceasing."* - 1 Thessalonians 5:17

Love by trusting without surveillance, for I am working even when you cannot see. *"Now faith is the assurance of things hoped for, the conviction of things not seen."* - Hebrews 11:1

Love by hoping without guarantees, for your hope is not in your spouse's change but in My faithfulness. *"May the God of hope fill you with all joy and peace in believing, so that you may abound in hope by the power of the Holy Spirit."* - Romans 15:13

Love by believing without proof, for I am doing a new thing in your marriage that eyes have not seen. *"But, as it is written, 'What no eye has seen, nor ear heard, nor the human heart conceived, what God has prepared for those who love him'"* - 1 Corinthians 2:9

Love by surrendering without fear, for perfect love casts out fear, and I am perfect love. *"There is no fear in love, but perfect love casts out fear."* - 1 John 4:18

Love by resting without anxiety, for I am the one who works while you rest. *"Come to me, all you that are weary and are carrying heavy burdens, and I will give you rest."* - Matthew 11:28

Love by prayer without control, for I am the one who hears and answers in My time. *"Do not worry about anything, but in everything by prayer and supplication with thanksgiving let your requests be made known to God."* - Philippians 4:6

A HEALING PRAYER FROM JESUS:

My precious child, as you close this book and step into this new way of loving, receive My blessing over your marriage:

I am healing the wounds that have made you grasp so tightly. I am replacing your need to control with confidence in My control. I am transforming your anxiety about your spouse into expectancy for what I will do.

I am working in your spouse's heart right now, even as you read these words. The prayers you have prayed, the tears you have shed, the surrender you have offered—none of it has been wasted. I am weaving it all together for a love story that will bring glory to My name.

I am giving you new eyes to see your spouse as I see them—not as a project to be completed, but as My beloved child on their own journey toward Me. I am teaching you to love with My love, which never fails, never gives up, and never runs out.

Rest now in My perfect love. Trust Me with the spouse I have given you. Watch Me do what only I can do. Your marriage is safe in My hands, and so are you.

I love you. I love your spouse. I love your marriage. And I am not finished with your story.

Go now and love as I have loved you.

Amen.

"And now faith, hope, and love abide, these three; and the greatest of these is love."- 1 Corinthians 13:13

The journey of letting go and letting God never truly ends—it only deepens. Each day brings new opportunities to choose trust over control, prayer over pressure, and surrender over striving. You now have the tools. You have learned the secret. The rest of your marriage story is waiting to be written by the One who authors perfect love stories.

Let go. Let God. And watch Him write yours.

THE RED THREAD

A Symbol of Sacred Surrender

The red thread on this book's cover draws from the powerful biblical story of Rahab and the scarlet cord found in the Book of Joshua. When Israelite spies came to scout the city of Jericho before its conquest, a woman named Rahab chose to protect them rather than turn them over to her king.

In return for her courage, the spies instructed Rahab to tie a scarlet cord from her window as a sign of protection. When the walls of Jericho fell, every building was destroyed—except the house marked by the red cord. Rahab and her family were saved because she chose to trust in God's promise rather than rely on her own understanding.

The scarlet cord represents the ultimate act of "letting go and letting God." Rahab had to release control of her circumstances, surrender her own plans for safety, and place her complete trust in

God's protection. The red thread became her lifeline—not because of anything she could do, but because of what God promised to do.

For Christians across all traditions, this story foreshadows the redemption found in Christ's blood. Just as Rahab trusted in the scarlet cord for deliverance, we are called to trust in God's promises when we cannot see the outcome. The red thread reminds us that sometimes the most powerful thing we can do is to let go of our need to control and trust that God's protection covers us, even when everything around us seems to be falling apart.

The red thread is a daily reminder that your transformation, your spouse's growth, and the future of your marriage do not rest on your ability to manage every detail, but on God's faithful promises to those who trust in Him.

ABOUT THE AUTHORS

Two Couples Serving Together in Marriage Ministry Became the Dearest of Friends

*T*he wisdom shared in this book comes not from academic theory but from decades of real-world experience ministering to couples on the brink of divorce who discovered that when human strategies fail, divine intervention succeeds. The authors' philosophy is simple yet revolutionary: the most powerful tool in saving a marriage isn't found in any counseling or communication technique—it's found in letting go and letting God work.

Steve and Leigh Baumann
The Baumanns have dedicated nearly two decades to transforming marriages through their work as presenters at Rediscovery Retrouvaille marriage retreats. Their expertise in marriage ministry has gained international recognition, highlighted when asked to share

their methods of ministering to struggling couples as guests of Pope Francis at the World Meeting of Families in Dublin, Ireland.

As prolific authors and curriculum developers, the Baumanns have created comprehensive resources for couples at every stage of their marriage journey. Their written works include "The Marriage Tune Up" and "The Invisible Rule Book to be Married to Me," series, while their curriculum development spans the "Marriage Recovery" program, a 12-step marriage support program, and the "Six Weeks to Us Marriage Master Class" available in an online webinar format. They are also co-writers of the "Discipleship for Couples" weekend retreat curriculum and developers of the innovative "Deep Trait Personality Assessment for Couples". The Baumanns are a sought-after voices in marriage ministry, as their approach combines practical wisdom with spiritual insight, helping couples navigate the complexities of marriage with personal authenticity.

Beyond their writing and speaking, Steve and Leigh serve in a global leadership capacity with Marriage Rediscovery Ministries, spearheading efforts to expand marriage ministry throughout the United States and Canada. Their influence extends internationally as they present and speak frequently on a comprehensive range of marriage topics suitable for marriages in all stages, including Marriage Conflict Management, Emotional Intelligence, Stewardship in Ministry, Faith Formation, Couple Mentoring and Discipleship for Couples.

Steve and Leigh's philosophy centers on the strength of peer ministry, believing that couples who have experienced disconnection and found their way back to reconnection are uniquely qualified to help others.

Their focus is on helping couples become healthy, stable family units, bringing families back together, and back to their faith. Through their extensive work with struggling marriages, they have witnessed countless couples move from the brink of divorce to renewed intimacy and partnership, proving that even the most damaged relationships can be restored with God's help. They are constantly in awe of how God as worked in their own marriage.

Bill and Trudy Hehn

The Hehns have dedicated over four decades to strengthening marriages through their ministry work with thousands of struggling couples. As founding members of the Rediscovery Retrouvaille ministry in Jacksonville, Florida, they have witnessed firsthand the transformative power of surrender in marriage—a discovery that revolutionized not only their own relationship but their entire approach to helping others.

Their expertise extends far beyond their local community. Bill and Trudy are sought-after speakers who present nationwide on marriage and faith-related topics, including forgiveness, faith formation, discipleship, and ministry service. Their influence has reached international levels as they have led efforts to develop marriage ministries worldwide and fostered the growth of the Rediscovery Retrouvaille movement across multiple continents.

As peer ministers, the Hehns have personally mentored thousands of couples through some of their darkest marital seasons. Their unique gift lies not in offering quick fixes or simple solutions, but in guiding couples toward the profound truth that lasting change comes through spiritual surrender rather than human effort. They have also devoted themselves to training the next generation of marriage ministers, mentoring numerous presenting couples and clergy who now carry marriage ministry forward around the globe. Their shared ministry mentality has been, "When you serve, your struggle becomes someone else's strength."

They continue to serve on the global leadership team for Marriage Rediscovery Ministries and speak regularly at marriage conferences, retreats, and seminars, always pointing couples toward the same liberating truth they've discovered: you can't change your spouse, but God can change everything.

Dedication
In grateful memory of Father Patrick (Paddy) Carroll, CSSp, our dear friend, mentor and supporter of many years. You were there at the beginning and you'll always be with us to the end. Your Irish warmth, humor and wisdom, along with your love and support of married couples through the ministry of Retrouvaille has sustained us through thick and thin and helped countless couples, including us, rediscover God's grace. You're missed beyond belief.
"Well done, good and faithful servant" – Mathew 25:21

- For Info About the Let Go and Let God Book Series or Speaking Engagements: **LetGoLetGodBooks.com**
- For Info About Rediscovery Retrouvaille Marriage Retreats, please visit **MarriageLifeline.org**
- To bring Six Weeks to Us Marriage Master Class, to your church or parish, visit **SixWeeksToUs.org**

www.ingramcontent.com/pod-product-compliance
Lightning Source LLC
Chambersburg PA
CBHW031424290426
44110CB00011B/511